ISBN (paperback) 978-1-7779906-9-5

Mercury Mouse

Written by Michael Allan and
Katie Allan
Illustrated by Katie Allan
Edited by Tracy Allan

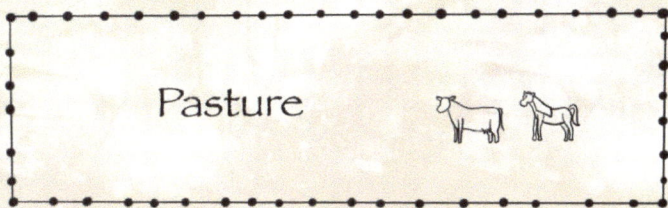

Pasture

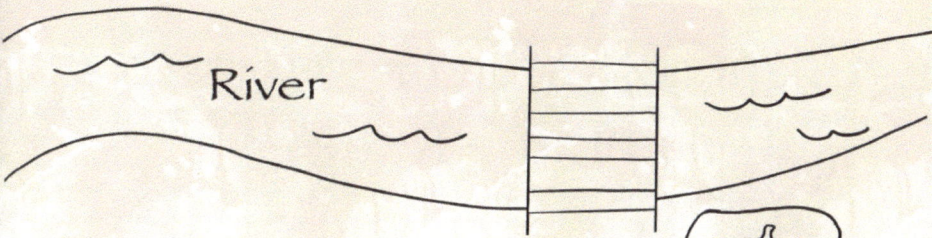

River

Lookout Hill

Duck Pond

Chicken Coop

Pig Pen

Vegetable Garden

Dodger's House

Barn

Mercury's Home

Farm House

Chapter 1: Mercury Mouse and Little Katie

In a small hole in the wall, along the floor of the kitchen, in a cozy nest, lived Mama Mouse and her baby, Mercury Mouse. From the time her baby was born, Mercury was fast. Before he could walk he was very curious and looked quickly from here to there, up and down. As soon as he was old enough to walk, he didn't walk, he ran. He ran everywhere checking things out, to see what they were. Mama Mouse could have named him Curiosity, but she didn't. She named him Mercury and it suited him perfectly.

3

One day Mercury Mouse went exploring in the kitchen. He went under the kitchen table looking for food. This was often a good place to find food so he went from chair to chair. Then, under one of the chairs, he found several crumbs and chunks of food!

Mercury picked up a big piece of broccoli. It was almost too big for him to carry. He ran back to his mama in their nest and said, "Look what I have! I found a jackpot of food!"

"This is marvelous," said Mama. "We will not be hungry tonight."

Mercury said, "If I bring back all the food that I have found, we will not be hungry for a week."

Mercury sped back and forth from the nest to the chair, each time bringing back more food for himself and his mama. On the last trip to the chair, Mercury picked up the last crumb, turned, and crashed into a shoe! Inside the shoe was a foot, the foot was connected to a leg, and the leg belonged to a girl! The girl looked very tall to Mercury, but to a mouse, pretty much everything looks tall. In reality, the girl was not tall. She was actually a small girl named Little Katie. Mercury had been gathering food from under her chair at the kitchen table.

Mercury Mouse was feeling woozy from the crash and his head seemed to spin. Then everything went dark and he fell over with a soft thump. Mercury did not hurt himself because a mouse has very short legs, so he did not have far to fall.

Little Katie looked down and saw Mercury. She said, "Oh no. Poor little guy." She bent down and picked up Mercury in her hand and began to pet him gently with her finger. Mercury woke up and thought, "This is kind of nice. I am snuggly, warm, and I am being cuddled. I like this."

Little Katie said to Mercury, "We need to find you a home."

Little Katie lived on a large, sprawling farm with her parents. She went outside to the big, red barn carrying Mercury in her hand. Just inside the barn door, she laid out some straw and hay in a corner, and made a small nest for Mercury. She carefully put Mercury down inside the nest and said, "From now on, this is your new home."

Mercury thought, "Wow. This is alright! Nice and soft, and so cozy." The curious Mercury looked around and he was amazed at how big the barn was. He had never been outside of the house before. He looked up. The ceiling was so high and the barn was so big that four kitchens could have fit in there. Mercury ran outside and he could not believe his eyes. The open space went on and on. There were fields and hills that went on as far as he could see. When he looked up, there was no ceiling!

The farm had all kinds of food. There were berries, seeds, grains, and other things that Mercury had not seen before, and they looked like they might be good to eat. He thought, "Mama will know if they are good to eat. My mama has to see this!" Mercury ran back to the house.

Little Katie called out, "Where are you going? Come back!"

Mercury swiftly ran into the kitchen to the nest and shouted excitedly, "Mama, Mama! You have to come with me and see something!"

Mama said, "Slow down Mercury, I am coming."

Mercury ran back outside toward the barn. Mama Mouse followed as fast as she could, but she could not keep up with Mercury. Out of breath, Mama finally caught up. Mercury said, "Look Mama, this is our new home. Little Katie made it for us!"

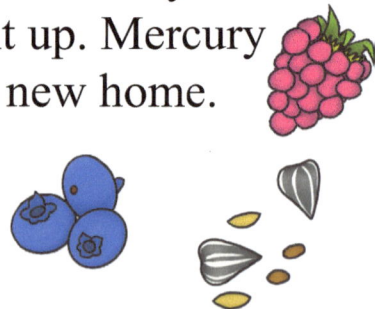

"This is a perfect home for us," said Mama. The two mice ran back to their nest behind the kitchen wall, picked up all of their belongings, and brought everything to their new home in the barn.

Mercury and Mama settled nicely into their new home. Mercury knew they would live happily on the farm for a long, long time.

Chapter 2: Mercury Mouse meets Darla the Dog

The next day Mercury thought he would explore his new world. He scampered out of the big barn and stopped to enjoy the warmth of the sun on his back. He looked up and again marveled that there was no ceiling. How glorious it was to see the bright, blue sky. Being so curious, he had to see what other wonders were waiting for him on the farm. Mercury turned right and ran around to the side of the barn. Right there in front of him was a small wooden house with a large opening in the front wall. The opening looked similar to a mouse hole, but much taller and wider. The mouse that could fit in there would come up to Little Katie's waist. That would be a big mouse!

Mercury quickly took two steps forward and sniffed the air. It was a strange smell, unlike anything he had smelled before. He crept closer and sniffed again. Nothing smelled dangerous, so Mercury thought he would go inside the small house to explore further.

As he tried to step forward, he realized that he couldn't move. Something was holding him back. Mercury turned his head and saw a giant paw standing on his tail. He gazed up and a big, furry animal with floppy ears was staring down at him.

The animal said, "Who are you?"

Mercury timidly replied, "I…I…I am Mercury Mouse."

The animal said, "Hello, Mercury Mouse! I am Darla the Dog. What do you do here?"

"Ah…ah, I explore and I look for food. What do you do here?" asked Mercury.

Darla proudly responded, "I'm the boss around here. I practically run the farm. I only take orders from Little Katie."

Of course, the farm was really managed by Katie's mom and dad, but Darla did not know that. In fact, she didn't even know all of the work that it took to operate a farm. Little Katie fed Darla the Dog and took care of her, and occasionally she gave Darla some tasks to do around the farm like herding the sheep or bringing in the cows. Darla thought Little Katie was the one who ran the farm, and that she must be second in command.

"Pleased to meet you, Darla," proclaimed Mercury. He was feeling more comfortable now. "Little Katie gave my mama and me a new home in the barn."

"Well," said Darla, "that's great. We will have to find a job for you to do on the farm. How does that sound?"

Mercury was excited. He had never had a job before. He wasn't even sure what that meant, but being so curious he was willing to try it.

Darla said, "I see that you were about to go into my doghouse."

"This is your house?" exclaimed Mercury. Well, that explained why the door was so big. It was large enough for Darla to fit through.

"Come inside," said Darla. She was happy to invite her new friend into her home.

The two went into Darla's doghouse. Inside there was straw on the ground and a blanket in the corner for Darla to keep warm on cold nights. In the opposite corner were a bowl of water and a bowl of food.

Darla the Dog said, "Help yourself to some water. In fact, you and your mama can come over anytime when you need a drink. My door is always open."

Mercury was very pleased to have a new friend. He was anxious to tell the news to Mama.

"Come on, Mercury. I will show you the rest of the farm. There is much, much more to see. Let's go to the top of Lookout Hill. You can see the whole farm from there," said Darla.

Darla started to run toward Lookout Hill, and Mercury followed her. After about one minute, Mercury realized that even though he was fast for a mouse, his tiny little legs were no match for the big, long legs of a full-sized dog. Mercury cried out, "Wait, Darla. I can't keep up!"

Darla stopped and looked around, wondering what the problem could be. She wasn't even warmed up yet.

"How am I ever going to make it all the way up to the top of that hill?" panted Mercury. All of a sudden the hill looked much farther away and much higher.

Darla said, "I have an idea. You do not have to run up the hill. Climb up my leg and you can ride on my back."

To Mercury, that sounded like a fun and exciting way to get to the top of the hill! Mercury ran up Darla's leg and onto her back. Mercury was so light, Darla could barely feel him on her back.

Darla said, "Are you ready? Hang on tight!" Darla bounded up the hill.

Poor Mercury was getting tossed from left to right, and up and down. Mercury grasped Darla's fur with his tiny paws and held on tightly. Mercury was getting used to the ride. Actually, it was kind of fun!

Together they made it to the top of Lookout Hill.

Darla asked, "Well, what do you think?"

From the top of the hill, Mercury could see the entire farm. He could not believe how huge it was! It went on and on. Behind the barn was a chicken pen and coop. Several chickens were pecking at the ground with a rooster looking over them. Next to the chicken pen was a pond with several ducks. Beyond the pond was the pigsty with several pigs eating at their trough. In the distance, he could see cows and horses grazing in the pasture. On the other side of the farm were a grainfield, a cornfield, and a vegetable garden.

Mercury said in amazement, "This farm is so big, it will take me a lifetime to explore everything."

Darla the Dog replied, "I've got it. I know what your new job should be. While you are exploring the farm, you can look for things that need to be fixed or improved for the animals, and report back to me. I will make things right again, and don't worry, with you on my back, we can explore the whole farm in no time!"

That is how Mercury got his new job and how Darla the Dog and Mercury Mouse became best friends.

Chapter 3: Mercury Mouse and Buster the Cat

The next morning, Mercury woke up and stretched. It was a beautiful day on the farm. "Today, I will continue to explore the farm and meet with the other animals," thought Mercury.

Mercury ran out of the barn and turned left. He had not yet turned left coming out of the barn. Up until now, he only went right where Darla the Dog lived in her doghouse.

When Mercury rounded the corner, he saw an enormous pile of chopped wood stacked up against the barn wall. There were lots of little holes and crevices in the wood. "That could be fun to explore," thought Mercury.

Just beyond the woodpile was a little house that was not quite as big as Darla's doghouse. Mercury was curious about the little house, so he moved closer to check it out. When he got close enough to see inside, his heart began to beat very fast. Mercury stopped in his tracks.

There was a very fierce-looking cat sleeping inside the little house!

Mercury Mouse started to back up very slowly and quietly, but that did not work. The orange cat sniffed the air with his eyes still closed. Then the cat's eyes opened wide! The cat saw Mercury and looked at him with an evil smile.

Mercury panicked and took off for the woodpile! He ran as fast as he could into the first hole he could find. The hole was much too small for the cat to get into.

Mercury quickly scrambled to the back of the woodpile until he reached the barn wall. There was nowhere to go. Mercury turned around and peaked out of the front of the hole. All he could see was a big cat eye staring back at him.

Once again, Mercury searched for an escape route, but he couldn't find a way to get out. The only way out was the way he came in, and that was blocked by the cat!

With an evil laugh, the cat declared, "Come out, come out little mouse. I will not hurt you!"

Mercury stayed in the woodpile, trembling with fear.

The cat did not move and said, "I am Buster the Cat. I am new on the farm and I just want to be your friend. Come out where I can catch you, oops... I mean, come out where I can talk to you."

Still trembling, Mercury said, "I can talk from here. I don't need to come out."

Buster realized that Mercury was too smart

for his tricks and he knew that Mercury would not come out. Buster squeezed one of his paws through the hole and into the woodpile! He came close to Mercury, but he could not reach him. Mercury was safe for now, but how would he get out?

Buster was determined to catch Mercury. He meowed wildly as he continued to stretch and reach his paw inside the woodpile!

Darla the Dog heard the commotion and ran to investigate. When Buster saw Darla running toward him, he quickly pulled his paw out of the hole in the woodpile. In his panic, Buster caught his paw on a sliver of wood and he cried out in pain!

Buster backed up and explained, "I wasn't going to hurt the mouse. I was just playing."

Darla announced, "Mercury Mouse is my friend. You will never hurt Mercury or any other creature on this farm. On this farm, we are all one big happy family and family helps and supports family. Now promise me that you will never pick on Mercury Mouse again."

Buster the Cat, still in pain, whimpered, "I promise that I will never hurt Mercury. But… my paw hurts!"

Mercury popped his head out of the hole and said, "I think I can help you with that."

Mercury ran over to Buster's paw and gently bit onto the end of the sharp sliver of wood, and then pulled it out.

Buster's paw immediately felt better. "Thank you, Mercury. It is nice that family help each other. I am sorry for chasing you."

Mercury and Buster did not become best friends, but they always respected and helped each other from that time on.

Chapter 4: Buster returns the Favor

Buster the Cat was sitting on the ledge of the little window at the top of the barn. The farmer used this window to pull the heavy bales of hay up to the loft of the barn for storage. The loft would be the second floor or upstairs in a house, but a barn does not have stairs to the second floor. Instead of stairs going to the second floor, it has a ladder. It also has a rope hanging from a pulley on top of the little window that Buster was looking out of.

Buster, like all cats, was curious. He liked to see what was going on around him. From the high window of the barn he could see everything. He could see the chicken pen, the pond and the pigsty. Further out past the river, he could see the green pasture where the cows and horses roam and graze for food.

Buster could even see Mercury coming back from the pasture. Mercury was exploring the farm, as he usually did.

Just then, a shadow quickly passed over Mercury and then it disappeared. Mercury thought that it must have been a small cloud to pass by so quickly.

Up until a few days ago, Mercury lived in Katie's house and had never been outside, so he did not yet understand the movement of the clouds and the sun all that well.

There it was again, a shadow that passed over very quickly. "That is very strange," thought Mercury.

Up in the sky, a hawk was circling over the farm, looking for mice to eat for supper.

From the window Buster could see the hawk and Mercury Mouse. The hawk had not yet seen Mercury running through the field. Buster cried out to Mercury, "Look up, there is a hawk circling above you!"

Mercury could not hear Buster because he was too far away.

"I have to save Mercury," thought Buster. Buster jumped out of the window and caught the rope. He swiftly climbed down to the ground and started running toward Mercury, calling Mercury's name all the way.

At the same time, the hawk spotted Mercury in the tall grass. He circled around one more time and lined up Mercury in his sights. Then he started his steep dive, straight down toward Mercury!

Mercury still had no idea what was going on.

Buster was getting closer and closer to
Mercury, but so was the hawk. Buster cried
out, "Look out!"

Mercury stopped and looked up. He saw the hawk heading right for him. Mercury froze in his tracks. That was his only defense. He thought that if he didn't move, then the hawk may not see him.

The hawk was just about to snatch up Mercury when suddenly, whomp!

Buster leapt up and pushed the hawk away just as the hawk's talons brushed Mercury's fur. Buster the Cat knocked the hawk to the ground. The hawk was shocked and a little dazed.

Buster shouted at the hawk, "Mercury is part of the farm family. We all help and protect each other on the farm. Go away and fly somewhere else!"

The hawk flew up into the air and as he left he said, "I am never coming back here again. There are many other places for me to find supper more easily."

Mercury Mouse felt great relief and thanked Buster many times for saving him.

Buster said, "No problem. You helped me before, and I am glad that I could return the favor."

Chapter 5: The Fox and the Chickens

The next day Mercury thought, "It is time to visit the chickens. I will introduce myself, tell them what my job is on the farm, and I will ask if they need anything to be corrected."

Mercury ran out of the barn and turned right. Then he ran past the doghouse to the back of the barn. Just beyond the barn were the chicken pen and chicken coop.

The chicken pen was surrounded by a wire fence. At the end of the fenced pen was the chicken coop, or henhouse, where the chickens would go inside to lay eggs and to sleep at night.

Mercury squeezed through one of the small holes in the wire fence. He immediately saw all kinds of food on the ground inside the pen. There were corn kernels, wheat, chicken feed and vegetable greens. Mercury picked out a nice big kernel of corn. As soon as he picked it up, a hen came racing toward him, flapping her wings and screaming, "Balk, balk, balk, balk!"

Mercury looked up and said, "What's going on?"

The hen declared, "This is a safe place for the chickens. You are not a chicken, so you don't belong here. Everything inside the pen belongs to the chickens, including the food!"

Mercury dropped the kernel of corn. He explained, "I am just little and I don't eat much. My name is Mercury Mouse."

The hen flapped her wings and yelled, "Get out! You don't belong here!"

Mercury was feeling stressed and he wasn't sure what to do. This was not going as he had planned. Mercury looked around and saw a big rooster watching over the pen from the top of a fence post.

Mercury thought he might have better luck talking to the rooster. He seemed to be much calmer. Mercury ran up to the top of the fence post.

The big rooster looked at Mercury Mouse and said calmly, "I see that you met Henimay Hen. Did you learn a lesson?"

Mercury Mouse replied, "Gosh, did I ever. Don't mess with the chickens!"

"I am Rex Rooster. What is your name?" said the big rooster.

"I am Mercury Mouse. Darla the Dog gave me the job of talking to all the farm animals to see if everything is going well. If something isn't going well, then I report back to Darla and she corrects it."

Rex Rooster said, "You came to the right place. We have some things that are not the way that they should be."

Mercury wanted to help the chickens, and this could show Darla how useful he could be on the farm! "What is bothering the chickens?" asked Mercury.

Rex explained, "There is a sly fox that is creeping around the chicken pen and he is up to no good! The fox is trying to sneak into the pen through that hole in the fence." Rex pointed with his wing to a place in the fence where the wire was broken and pulled back,

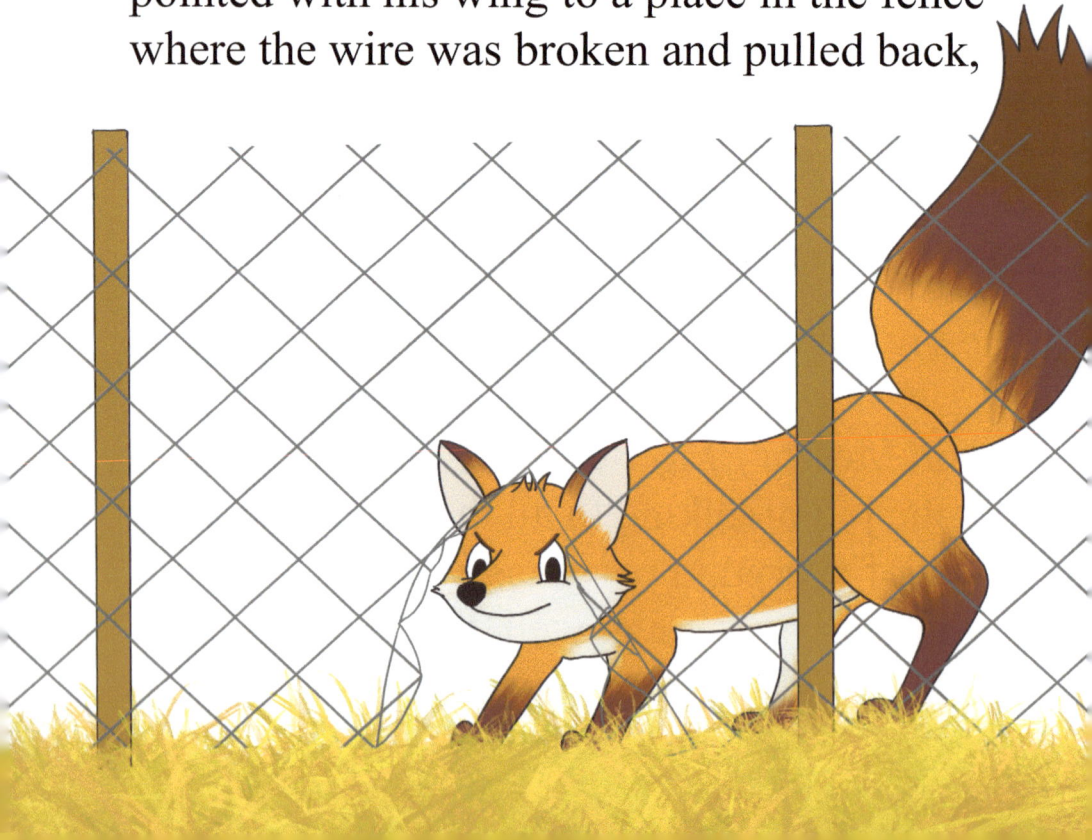

exposing a hole large enough for a fox to fit through.

Mercury now understood why Henimay Hen was so angry and protective of the chicken pen. Mercury declared, "Don't worry. I know exactly what to do!"

Mercury ran down the fence post and quickly sprinted straight to Darla the Dog. "Come quickly, Darla! There is a fox that is bothering the chickens, and they are scared!"

Darla the Dog said, "Hop on my back, Mercury. There is no time to waste." Darla charged full speed to the chicken pen with Mercury hanging on for dear life.

They quickly arrived at the chicken pen and Mercury hopped off of Darla's back. Darla sniffed around the outside of the pen and immediately tracked down the fox, which was hiding behind the chicken coop. She began to chase after the fox, but the fox saw Darla coming!

The fox was shocked and his eyes grew wide as Darla bounded toward him. The fox knew he was in trouble! He turned and ran with Darla chasing after him. The fox darted through the vegetable garden and then through the pasture.

Darla kept pace with the fox, barking as she chased the fox away from the chicken pen.

The fox ran to the back of the pasture and under the fence to the neighboring field. Darla stopped at the fence, but she kept barking. The fox kept running and running, and was never seen again.

Meanwhile, back at the chicken pen, Little Katie was arriving to feed the chickens with a basket of seeds and grains.

Mercury ran up to Little Katie.

Little Katie looked down at Mercury Mouse and said, "Hello, Mercury. How nice to see you."

Mercury ran to the hole in the fence and bounced up and down, while pointing to the hole and looking frantically back at Little Katie.

Little Katie said, "Oh my! You found a hole in the fence. I will try to fix it to protect the chickens. Thank you for pointing that out to me, Mercury."

Little Katie put down the basket and knelt beside the fence. She bent the fence to cover the hole, then she twisted the wire together to hold it in place. "There," she said, "it's all fixed and good as new!"

Mercury ran over to Rex Rooster and Henimay Hen.

Rex said, "Thank you to you and Darla the Dog for getting rid of that pesky fox!"

Henimay Hen added, "And thanks for getting the fence fixed. You are always welcome here to visit the chickens. Anytime you need a snack, you can come by and visit us. Little Katie always ensures that we have plenty of food."

Henimay picked up the largest kernel of corn and gave it to Mercury as a reward.

Chapter 6: Candace Cow

The following day, Mercury decided to go for a walk a bit farther from his barn. When he was on Lookout Hill with Darla, he saw a large pasture with lots of grass and hay. He wanted to explore this pasture to see what new adventures awaited him.

Mercury walked up the big hill and then down the other side. The pasture was huge! It was surrounded by a wooden fence and several cows were grazing in the grass. Some of the cows were white with big black spots, and some were all brown.

Mercury was a little nervous because the cows were much larger than he thought they would be, but being so brave he scooted under the fence to get closer to the herd. All of a sudden, a large hoof landed next to him with a loud thud! And then another hoof! Mercury ran as fast as he could and looked back to see that one of the black and white cows had almost stepped on him! But this animal looked sad. Mercury wanted to help and said, "Hey! I'm Mercury Mouse! What's wrong?"

44

The animal looked at him with tears in her
eyes and said, "Oh, I'm sorry! I didn't see
you there. I'm Candace Cow, but my friends
call me Candy. I'm just trying to find my bell.
It fell off of my neck, and now I can't find it."

Mercury, being short and close to the ground, was an expert at finding things. He searched all around and finally saw the shiny, gold bell glistening in the grass, just on the other side of the fence. "Candy! I found it! It's over there!" He pointed to the other side of the fence.

Candy strolled over and realized that her bell must have fallen off when she was looking over the fence. Unfortunately, she could not reach over the fence and down to the grass to pick up her bell. "Oh no," she cried, "I'm never going to get it back."

"Don't worry," said Mercury, "I can fit under the fence and get it for you!" Mercury ran under the fence and pushed the gold bell back to Candy's side of the fence so she could pick it up.

Candy was thrilled! She quickly put her bell back on and shook her head from side to side so that the bell rang loud, for all to hear! "Wow, Mercury, you're my new best friend! I am going to tell all the cows to watch out for you and your family, and no one will ever come close to stepping on you again! Come to visit us anytime."

Mercury had a good feeling inside him because even though he was a tiny mouse, he was able to help Candy to get her bell back and help her to feel better.

Candy continued, "Why don't you come to meet my friends!" She took Mercury over to meet more animals in the pasture. These are my friends Cora Cow and Chloe Cow, and this is our friend, Horace Horse. He's a racing horse so he can run really, really fast!

Horace was thrilled to meet such a tiny mouse and said, "Hey Mercury, I saw what you did for Candy. You are so kind! Do you want to go for a ride?"

Mercury climbed up the horse's back leg and across his back so he could hold onto his long, smooth mane.

"Hold on tight!" shouted Horace as he started to run.

Mercury almost fell off, and had to grip the mane with all of his strength to stay on

Horace's back. What a thrilling ride for little Mercury! He was able to see so much of the farm. With the wind blowing in his face, so high above the pasture, he felt like he was flying!!

Chapter 7: Mercury Goes Swimming in The Mud

The next morning, Mercury decided to visit the pigs at the pigsty. He went past the chicken pen calling out, "Hello, Henimay. Hello, Rex."

Henimay Hen replied, "How lovely to see you Mercury. Where are you off to today?" Mercury exclaimed, "I am going to visit the pigs."

Henimay Hen replied with a chuckle, "Oh, that will be fun. Those piglets are a happy bunch!"

Mercury arrived at the pigsty and climbed up to the top of a fence post. The post was completely covered in slippery mud.

Mercury looked into the pigsty below and saw the three little piglets snorting and lazing in a large puddle of mud. Mercury called out, "Good morning. I am Mercury Mouse. What are your names?"

The first piglet said, "I am Piglet One."

The next piglet said, "I am Piglet Two."

The last piglet said, "I am Leonard."

"Leonard?" questioned Mercury. "Why not Piglet Three?"

Leonard replied, "Pigs only have two toes on their hooves, so it is difficult for a pig to count past two."

"That makes sense to me," thought Mercury.

Before Mercury could say anything else, he lost his footing on the slippery post and fell belly first into the thick, brown mud! The three piglets all burst out laughing at the same time! Thinking that Mercury had come to play with them, they all jumped up and belly-flopped into the mud. Each time a piglet splashed down, a wave of mud rippled through the puddle. Mercury was pushed away on the top of the wave of mud like a surfer! With the next splash, he was pushed back the other way. He was getting tossed around like a cork in the ocean. The piglets were laughing and snorting, and having a great time!

Mercury was not so sure that this was much fun for him!

Mama Pig heard all the laughing and splashing and decided to check on her piglets. When she saw poor little Mercury bobbing around in the mud she said, "Okay kids, that is enough. That little mouse is getting bounced around too much."

Piglet One said, "Aww, Mama. We were just having fun. This is our new friend, Mercury!"

Mama Pig turned to Mercury, "It's so nice to meet you Mercury. Welcome to our pigsty." Then Mama Pig explained to the piglets, "It is time for breakfast. Take Mercury and go down to the river to get washed. Then you can all come back here to eat."

Mercury tried to get his footing but he couldn't. He tried to swim out of the mud puddle, but that didn't work either. The mud was just too slippery and thick.

Piglet Two said, "Look, Mercury can't get

out!"

The three piglets laughed and snorted again. Leonard said, "Climb onto my back and I will carry you."

Mercury tried to get a grip but Leonard was too slippery. Piglets have very, very short hair, unlike the fur that Darla the Dog has.

Leonard said, "Don't worry Mercury. I will get you out."

Leonard gently bit down on Mercury's tail and picked him up. The other piglets both cheered!

Then, Piglet One called out, "Come on, let's go to the river. The last one in is a dirty piglet!"

With those words, they all raced down to the river with Mercury dangling from Leonard's mouth.

When they approached the shallow river, the three piglets carefully waded in. Then they dunked their heads in the water to wash their faces and ears. Mercury, still dangling from Leonard's mouth, was completely soaked, but he was finally clean.

The gang all trotted back to the pigsty for breakfast. The pigs all lined up at the food trough. Leonard placed Mercury on the rim of the trough. Then he dipped his snout into the trough, scooped out a portion of slop, and plopped it beside Mercury on the rim of the trough.

"Try it, Mercury, you might like it," said Mama Pig.

Mercury had never eaten anything that looked like that before, but he was always willing to try any new food. He sniffed at it. It smelled good! He tasted a small bite. It tasted like stew! Mercury said, "I do, I do like it!"

The pigs all laughed and cheered, and began to eat.

After breakfast, Mercury said, "Well, I see that everything is good here. I have to go home now so that my mama does not worry."

The piglets snorted and yelled out, "Come back anytime, Mercury. In fact, come back all the time!" They all laughed again.

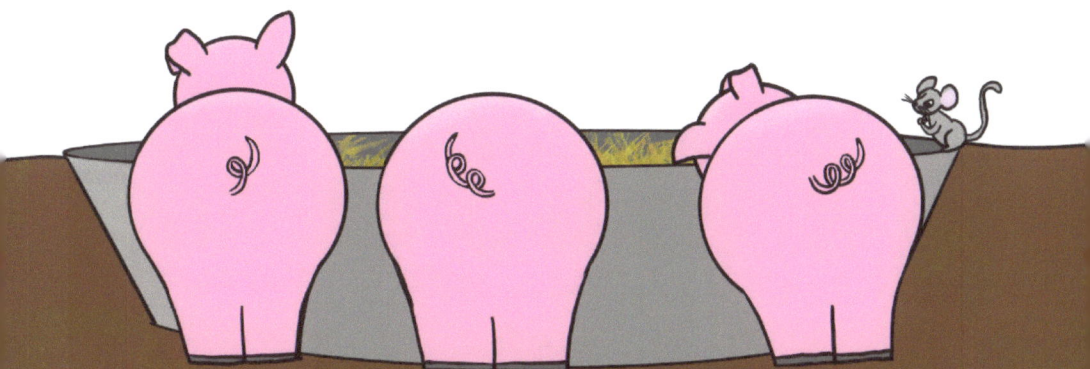

As Mercury walked back to his nest in the barn, he thought back to all of the new experiences he had during his first week outside of the house. Mercury and his mama got a terrific new home from Little Katie. He met new friends, Darla the Dog, Horace Horse, the cows Candace, Cora and Chloe, Rex Rooster and Henimay Hen. He had some hair-raising adventures with Buster the Cat, the hawk and the pesky fox. Then, finally, the muddy antics with the fun-loving piglets.

What a wonderful week! All was right with Mercury's new world! He was thrilled to be part of the farm family and he looked forward to more adventures!!

www.ingramcontent.com/pod-product-compliance
Lightning Source LLC
LaVergne TN
LVHW010030070426
835508LV00005B/286